LINCOLN MURDOCH

SEE YOU AT THE

Finish!

Tom – Keep
running the race
brother – looking to
Jesus!
II Tim. 4:7
Lincoln

See You at the Finish!

Lincoln Murdoch

ISBN 1-929478-36-4

Cross Training Publishing
317 West Second Street
Grand Island, NE 68801
(308) 384-5762

This book is manufactured in the United States of America.

Library of Congress Cataloging in Publication Data in Progress.

Published by Cross Training Publishing,
317 West Second Street
Grand Island, NE 68801

S E E   Y O U   A T   T H E *Finish!*

DEDICATION

This book is lovingly dedicated to the memory of my father-in-law, Larry D. Giles, Sr., who crossed the finish line June 14, 2001, having run a race that brought much glory to His Lord and Savior, Jesus Christ.

SEE YOU AT THE *Finish!*

ACKNOWLEDGEMENTS

I want to thank my wonderful wife, Jennifer, for her thoughtful input and proofreading and for her steady encouragement throughout this project. Thanks for being my Ironmate all these years and for being my running partner for life. I love you.

Thanks to Debbie Harmsen, who has been a catalyst for this book. Debbie, if it weren't for you, this would be nothing more than another idea that never became reality. Thanks for your watchful eye and for the wonderful way you let the Lord shine through you so transparently. You are world-class!

To David Yates and Randi McGee, I say another big "Thank You" for your input and thought on this book. Each of you bring a unique slant that has been very helpful to me. It's a joy to know you both.

Thanks to the Fellowship of Christian Athletes for the great work that you do year in and year out. Keep up the great work.

Finally, thanks goes to my friend, mentor, pastor, fishing buddy and father, Elmer Murdoch, and my wonderful mother Nancy Murdoch. Thanks for your editing, thoughts, prayers and constant encouragement on this project and throughout life. You both running your race the way I want to run mine, setting a good pace for those coming behind you. May you run for many more years.

SEE YOU AT THE *Finish!*

CONTENTS

S E E   Y O U   A T   T H E
Finish!

"Remember those earlier days after you had received the light, when you stood your ground in a great contest in the face of suffering. Sometimes you were publicly exposed to insult and persecution; at other times you stood side by side with those who were so treated. You sympathized with those in prison and joyfully accepted the confiscation of your property because you knew that you yourselves had better and lasting possessions. So do not throw away your confidence; it will be richly rewarded. **You have need of endurance, so that when you have done the will of God, you will receive what He has promised."**

Hebrews 10:32-36

INTRODUCTION

Stamp collecting, fishing, hunting, scrapbooking, coin collecting, gardening, skateboarding, woodworking, hang gliding, collecting baseball cards and model rocketry are all hobbies people enjoy. I have a hobby. Most folks think it's a bit strange and many don't understand how I can enjoy it, but I do. My hobby is endurance racing. Running, biking and swimming long distances—sometimes doing all three in one race.

Over the past 20-plus years, I have competed in many long-distance endurance races. I've finished 26.2 mile marathons, several 31 and 50 mile ultra marathons, and many triathlons, including two 70-mile triathlons and two 140-mile Ironman triathlons. (An Ironman triathlon consists of a 2.4-mile open water swim, followed by a 112-mile bike ride and finally a 26.2-mile marathon…all back to back on the same day.)

As a long-distance athlete, I know that endurance is a key component to every race. Without endurance, athletes cannot receive the finisher's prize at the end of the race. Without endurance, athletes may not even finish the race. The same is true for many sports. How many times have you seen football or basketball teams fall apart in the fourth quarter and lose because they didn't have the equivalent level of endurance and conditioning as that of their opponent?

As a Christian, I know I need endurance in my spiritual walk as well. Without endurance, we cannot receive the prize

God has for us in the end. Without endurance, we may not even finish the race God has marked out for us.

It's a sobering reality that there are Christians today who by next year will have drifted away from their faith, as mentioned in Hebrews 2:1. There are Christians in churches today who in a year will no longer be active in a church. There are Christians who are married today who will no longer be married a year from now. There are some that will have strayed away because they will have placed a higher value on worldly success or status, or because they have given in to peer pressure. Others will have been tempted to fall back due to a long-term struggle with an illness, an unanswered prayer, the death of a child or the incredible stress of being a single parent.

One year from now, some will be barely hanging on because of relational struggles, burnout or a severe attack from Satan. Other challenges people may face include the inability to conquer areas of sin or addiction or wounding from a spiritual leader from which they can't seem to recover.

I served as a pastor for 18 years and can think of people in almost every one of these categories. People whom, rather than enduring, seemed to abandon their Christian walk when the race got too hard.

Demas, who is mentioned in Philemon verse 24 and Colossians 4:14 as a co-worker in the gospel with Paul, abandoned Paul and the work because he fell in love with the world and what it had to offer (2 Timothy 4:10).

However, Romans 8:37-39 speaks of the victory that can be ours: "No, in all these things we are more than conquerors through Him who loved us. For I am convinced that neither death nor life, neither angels nor demons, neither the present nor the future, nor any powers, neither height nor depth, nor anything else in all creation will be able to separate us from the love of God that is in Christ Jesus our Lord." Jude verse 24 speaks of the great power of God to keep us from falling–that is wonderful news.

In spite of this, you have probably seen Christians who struggle (don't we all at times?) and fail. Seems like it's in the news quite often. We hear of moral failure, financial failure or some other kind of major problem. Maybe you've wondered, "If it's happened to him or her, is there any hope for me? Can I make it to the finish line running strong?" You know yourself well and you know the challenges that you face.

There is hope for you. One of the keys is to learn and apply the principles of spiritual endurance. Luke 21:19 says, "By your endurance, you will gain your lives."

4:00 a.m. The alarm clock awakened me from a deep sleep. My first thought was, "Thank you Lord for a good night's sleep and for simply letting me be here." Hawaii. Kailua-Kona, Hawaii to be exact, in October. It could only mean one thing. The Hawaiian Ironman Triathlon World Championship. The big one! The one on TV. Some have said it's the toughest one-day endurance race in the world. I lay in bed for a minute thanking the Lord for this opportunity. Tens of thousands of triathletes from around the world want to be in this race each year. Only 1,500 are allowed in. They come from 50 different nations. The best in the world are in this race. Filled with last minute self-doubt, I asked myself, "What in the world are YOU doing here?"

I got up, started drinking water and fluid-replacement drinks. I ate a Power Bar and a bagel with peanut butter and a banana. I took a quick shower to help wake me up, collected my gear and with Jennifer, my wonderfully supportive wife, headed out the door into the pre-dawn darkness…

CHAPTER ONE
The Role of Endurance

"You have need of endurance." – *Hebrews 10:36*

For many years, I have marveled at feats of human endurance. In particular, I am drawn to ultra-distance events. There are non-stop bicycle races across America, swimming competitions across the 22-mile English Channel from France to England, and adventure races like the Eco-Challenge, a 350-mile multi-sport team effort that includes swimming, biking, trekking, mountain climbing, rappelling and white-water rafting to the finish line.

There is also the Western States 100. This is a 100-mile foot race where athletes run in freezing weather in the mountains and also in the scorching heat in the desert in the same race. Then there is the Ironman, which is an ultra-distance triathlon. And, as if that's not enough, in France they triple all those distances in the Triple Ironman. And, mind boggling as it may be, in Mexico there is a Decca Ironman (Ironman distance x 10) and a Double Decca Ironman, (Ironman distance x 20). Do the math. It comes out to swimming 48 miles, biking 2,240 miles, and then running 524 miles! It sounds like something from "Ripleys Believe It Or Not," but it's true. It takes the few intrepid competitors several weeks to finish.

The human body is truly an amazing creation. No question about it. Some of the feats in physical endurance that individuals have accomplished are remarkable:

- A 78-year-old man finishing a 140-mile Ironman triathlon.
- A 92-year-old man finishing the 26.2-mile Boston Marathon.
- An ultra-distance runner averaging 57 miles per day for seven weeks to win a 2,700-mile race.
- A man making a solo 1,670-mile trek across Antarctica in 1998 in winds up to 150 mph, all the while pulling behind him a 330-pound sled with his food and supplies.
- A 32-year-old *blind* man who climbed Mt. Everest, which, at over 29,000 feet, is the highest mountain in the world.

The spirit inside a person is an even more amazing creation of God than the human body. It, too, has the capability to endure. The Bible gives examples of men and women of faith who endured hardship for the sake of the Gospel. In Hebrews 12, we read of Christians who were tortured, put in prison, or faced death by the sword; others were jeered at and flogged. Despite the persecution and mistreatment, they endured.

Today, most of us have not had to face physical torture or imprisonment for our faith, but still, the Christian life is often like trying to finish an ultra-distance event. There are mountains to climb, rocks to jump over, rivers to cross and storms to pass through. You won't make it without endurance.

What is endurance?

Endurance is defined as, "The act or power of withstanding hardship or stress." In a physical race, you endure if you don't give up and make it to the finish. In the spiritual race, it's the same. You endure if you don't give up, but rather, make it to the end.

Romans 5:3-4 says that we can rejoice in our suffering because we know that suffering produces endurance, endurance produces character, and character produces hope. This shows us that endurance is an important link in the chain of Christian growth. If endurance is not there, the chain is broken.

When we endure, we reflect God's image. Romans 15:5 calls God a "God of endurance." Psalm 136 repeats the phrase, "His steadfast love *endures* forever" in 26 consecutive verses. He understands endurance because he is an enduring God and He lives in every believer by His Spirit to *be* his or her endurance source.

Hebrews 12:2-3 notes how Jesus showed us endurance when he "*endured* the cross." The verses also encourage us to "consider him who *endured* from sinners such hostility against himself, so that you might not grow weary of faintheartedness." Hebrews 6:15 states that "Abraham patiently *endured* and obtained the promise."

Warnings

The book of Hebrews is full of verses telling us not to give up and warning us about what happens if we do not endure. In Chapter 2, we are warned about drifting away from what we have heard. In Chapter 3, we are warned about going astray and having unbelief as well as being warned against the hardening of our hearts caused by continued sin.

Chapter 4 warns us against failure to reach God's place of rest. It also exhorts us to hold fast to our confession. Chapter 6 warns against being sluggish. It encourages us to seize the hope set before us.

Chapter 10 speaks of the righteous who shrink back and are destroyed. Chapter 13 says to not be led away by strange teachings.

We should not ignore these warnings. In general, warnings indicate that there is danger ahead, and we should take caution.

The Call to Endure

Balanced with all of these warnings in Hebrews is the call to endure. Hebrews 6:11 tells us to "show this same diligence to the very end." Hebrews 10:23 says, "Let us hold unswervingly to the hope we profess." Hebrews 12:7 challenges us to "endure hardship."

This brings us to our key verse, Hebrews 10:36, which says, "You have need of endurance…" The Greek word that is used for endurance in that verse means to "remain firm under pressure, to keep going under difficult circumstances." This word can be translated and is used elsewhere in the Bible as "persevere," "hold out," "stand firm," "bear up courageously," "don't give up," "keep right on," "stand your ground," "remain steadfast" and "meet the challenge."

The Rewards of Endurance

Hebrews 10:36 shows a good reason for enduring. It says, "You have need of endurance so that you might do the will of God." How many of us want to do the will of God? To do His will, we need endurance. It also says we'll "receive what is promised" if we endure.

The Bible records many other rewards for enduring. For example, if we endure
- we will be saved (Luke 21:19)
- we will reign with Jesus (2 Timothy 2:12)
- we will receive the crown of life (James 1:12)

Review

We need endurance. We have seen that when we endure we reflect the very image of God, and His character will be produced in us. Second, we have seen that if we don't endure, we can easily drift away from God's calling and destiny for our life. Third, we have seen that when we endure, we will still be running strong at the end as we run toward that grand finish line where we cross over from this earthly life into eternity with the Lord.

I was used to that early-morning alarm letting me know it was time to get going. For several months it had called me out of bed and onto my bike on Monday mornings (Mondays were my day off. Mondays are great days for pastors to take off after busy Sundays). Each Monday I'd ride a little farther than the last one. One week I'd ride my bike 60 miles, then the next week 70, and then 80, 90, 100. One hundred is a milestone. Cyclists refer to it as a century ride. In Hawaii it would be 112 miles, but not just miles. It would include climbing a volcano mountain with extreme heat and humidity–and wind. The Hawaii bike course is famous for its terrible winds known as the *ho'o mumuku* winds that numb the mind and can kill the spirit. They've been known to blow right in the athlete's faces at 40-50 strength-sapping miles per hour. Barren and desolate lava fields would be the landscape. How different than riding along Highway 92 in eastern Nebraska cutting a path through relatively flat cornfields mile after mile.

Most triathletes train 20-plus hours per week for several months leading up to an Ironman distance race. I barely had time for half of that. Every workout had to count. I'd try to do one long workout in each of the three disciplines each week, and then add in a second workout of a shorter distance in each of the disciplines. On Saturdays I'd do my long run, at the hottest, most humid time of the day to acclimate my body to those conditions. Sunday afternoons I'd try to get to the YMCA and get in my one long weekly swim of up to an hour and 15 minutes. Then, Mondays would bring my long ride.

The Ironman race is won (which, for most, is defined as just finishing) or lost during the months leading up to the race. The dedication and hard work before the race are what causes a person to become an Ironman. The race is just the icing on the cake. It confirms, "Yes, you did the work. You're an Ironman." But, would the amount of training I was able to get in be enough? Would the YMCA pool prepare me for a 2.4-mile open-ocean swim with 1,500 others splashing and kicking all around me? Would Nebraska Highway 92 sharpen my cycling skills enough to prepare me for 112 miles of the Queen K Highway that cuts its way through the moon-like landscape?

Three weeks before the race, on my last really long Monday ride of 110 miles, just a few miles from home, I pulled my quadriceps muscle. My heart hit the floor and then went through to the basement. I felt my hopes and dreams of finishing Hawaii go down the drain. Cindy, a physical therapist, worked hard on trying to get that muscle, the main muscle used in biking, treated and back to normal. But would it be? Only the Lord knew.

CHAPTER TWO

You Must Have a Plan

Commit your ways to the Lord and your plans will be established." – Proverbs 16:3

Before I begin any endurance race, I plan. I plan what equipment I'll need: running shoes and clothes, water bottles, Power Bars, swimming goggles, wetsuit, bike ready to roll, etc. I also plan how I am going to pace myself and reach my goals. Even before that, I have a training plan for the number of workouts and distances I'll need to cover over several months so I'll be able to finish a given race.

A few years ago my friend Gary and I ran a 50-mile foot race at Palo Duro Canyon just outside of Amarillo, Texas. We entered the race with a plan. We were going to run five miles, then walk 10 minutes; run four miles, then walk 10 minutes, run three miles, then walk 10 minutes; run two miles, then walk 10 minutes; run one mile, then walk 10 minutes. Then, we were going to run 10 minutes and walk 10 minutes all the way to the finish line…we hoped.

You don't go into an event like that without a plan. You

need a plan that is specific and measurable. Several months before the 140-mile Canadian Ironman Triathlon, I began to plot out my strategy. I laid out a training plan. I set goals for how long I would be in the water before I moved onto the bike ride, and then how fast I should bike so that I could finish that within a certain time frame, and then move onto the run. I wanted to finish the entire race in less than 13 hours. I couldn't have done it without a plan. Because I had a plan and followed it, I was able to finish more than an hour under my time goal.

It has been said "If you fail to plan, you plan to fail." This can be true in endurance sports, as well as in the Christian walk. If you aim at nothing, you're sure to hit it. We need to plan if we want to endure. We need to plan if we want to endure. Remember, it's Ready, Aim, Fire, not, Ready, Fire, Aim.

God Has Plans

There is nothing unspiritual about having a plan. God has plans. Psalm 33:11 says, "The plans of the Lord stand firm forever, the purposes of His heart through all generations." God has lots of plans—for you, for others, for the world.

God began creation with a plan. Genesis 1-2 clearly lays out how God had a seven-day plan for creating the universe. His plan for taking care of the Garden of Eden was to have Adam look after it. His plan for creating more human beings was for Adam and Eve to bear children. His plan for Adam and Eve and the animals to have food to eat was to give them vegetables and trees that bore fruit.

God has a plan for the nations and this world. In Isaiah 14:24 and 26, God says, "Surely, as I have planned, so it will be, and as I have purposed, so it will stand… This is the plan determined for the whole world."

Jeremiah 29:11 notes God's plans as well. "I know the plans I have for you, says the Lord, plans to prosper you and not to harm you, plans to give you hope and a future."

Ephesians 2:10 also talks about plans God has for us. "For we are God's workmanship, created in Christ Jesus to do good works, which God prepared in advance for us to do."

God has a plan for our salvation through Jesus and His sacrificial death on the cross. When Jesus came to Earth, He had a plan: Fulfill God's plan of saving us by dying on the cross and being resurrected.

God made us in His image. He wants us to follow His model of having plans. In fact, He expects us to make plans. Proverbs 16:3 says, "Commit your ways to the Lord and your plans will be established."

Do You Have a Plan?

- What is your plan for graduating with a certain grade point average?
- What is your plan for making the varsity team?
- What is your plan for a 50- to 60-year marriage that will grow stronger and get better each year?
- What is your plan for raising your children in Godliness?
- What is your plan for involvement and greater effectiveness in Kingdom ministry?
- What is your plan for being a good steward of your money? Your belongings? Your health?
- What is your plan for developing Godly character in your life?
- What is your plan for growing in God's Word?
- What is your plan for spiritual endurance?

How to Plan

First, take time to sit down and get before the Lord in prayer. Ask Him for a plan in a specific area where you want to grow. Listen to what He tells you. Write down what you feel He is saying to you.

God wants us to know His plans for us. Psalm 32:8 says, "I will instruct you and teach you in the way you should go." That is why it is important to pray first, then plan accordingly.

Secondly, in addition to prayer, the Bible informs us of God's plans for us and guides us in our planning. Psalm 119:105 says "Your word is a lamp to my feet and a light for my path." Be in His Word regularly and God will certainly be a lamp and a light to you.

Third, get the counsel of others older and wiser in the Lord than you are. Listen to them. Be accountable to them for carrying out your plan. Proverbs 15:22 says, "Without consultation, plans are frustrated, but with many counselors they succeed."

When we make plans in the light of Godly counsel, God's Word and what He reveals to us in prayer, we can trust Jesus with the results. Proverbs 3:6 attests to this: "In all your ways acknowledge Him and He will make your paths straight."

Plan big. Think big. Dream big. God's plans and destiny for you are much greater than what you are imagining right now.

Review:
Principle #1 – YOU MUST HAVE A PLAN

As Jennifer and I walked out into the darkness, we stepped into a flow of athletes all heading for the gate that opened at 5 a.m. and led into the main staging area. Through that gate would walk triathletes as young as 18 and as young at heart as 80. Athletes from the United States, Canada, Latin America, Europe and Asia could be heard speaking in their native languages. We got in line, waited, and finally, at 5 a.m., walked into the starting/transition area. Here, all the competitors had to have their race numbers marked on their arms and legs for easy identification. A friend who was way up in the Ironman corporation had given Jennifer a VIP pass so she could go in with me where most spectators could not. She waited patiently while I was marked. I then checked my bike, loaded it with my drink and food and checked the tires for proper pressure. She was definitely an "Iron-mate." She knew what this race meant to me, and I knew I'd be racing with her support, prayers and love.

After a quick kiss, I walked down the four or five stairs that led to what is called "Dig Me Beach," which is just a small patch of sand that leads to the ocean. I met up with several other Christians on the beach for a quick word of prayer, which was very encouraging. I gazed out across Kailua Bay, and my eyes followed the large orange buoys that marked the swim course. My heart sank a bit as I realized I couldn't see the last buoy. They just kept going and going, farther and farther out. Then, just a few minutes before the 7 a.m. cannon went off, I eased out into the water looking for a good starting spot. The pros were given a starting area up at the front a few yards ahead of all the rest of us. Suddenly the cannon exploded and 3,000 arms and 3,000 legs started churning up the ocean into a white foamy froth that made it difficult to see. The 1998 Hawaiian Ironman Triathlon was underway.

CHAPTER THREE

You Have to Have a Sense of Pace

"And don't grow weary in well doing..." – *Galatians 6:9*

Once you have a plan, it's time to get going. Only don't go too fast, but, then again, don't go out too slowly either. If you are going to endure, you can't go too fast because you are going to expend all your energy too quickly and burn out. If you go too slowly and dilly-dally around, your window of opportunity may pass you by.

I once heard a Christian leader say, "I'd rather burn out than rust out." I guess if I'm looking for a way to go *out*, I'd also rather burn out than rust out. But, I'm looking to stay *in* this spiritual race of life as long as I can. I certainly don't want to burn out, nor do I want to rust out. The issue is *in*. I want to stay *in* all the way to the finish.

Just as we find our pace in a long-distance event, we need to find a sense of pace in life. We need to move forward at a rate of speed that we can maintain for a lifetime.

Too Fast?

I once ran in a 10K (6.2-mile) road race with Frank Shorter, Olympic marathon gold medallist. I thought I'd do something a bit crazy. I got right up on the starting line with the world-class runners. There I was, standing right next to Frank Shorter. Wow! I wanted to see what it was like to run with Frank. So, the gun went off, Frank took off and so did I. The first 100 yards I was right with Frank. What a thrill to run side by side with one of the best runners the world has ever known. The second 100 yards, I was still with Frank though my body was trying to tell me something. I wasn't listening though, because I was running next to an Olympic gold medallist!

In the next couple of hundred yards my body was screaming at me to slow down. It was trying to tell me I'd probably not make it one mile at Frank's pace. I was spent. I started to fear that in the last mile of the race I'd be passed by very old men in black wingtip dress shoes with black socks, or elderly women in canvas Chuck Taylor high-top basketball shoes. Why? Because I went out too fast. (Here's a tip: In a foot race you know you've probably gone out too fast if everyone around you is speaking Swahili.)

I want to be a Christian when I'm 94. I want to love God more then than I do now. I want to remain in ministry as long as possible. But I must realize that if I go pedal-to-the-metal, full steam ahead all the time, I won't make it. In order to make it, I have to learn a sense of pace in my life.

You too may be tempted to go too fast. You plan to conquer all of life's mountains THIS week. You haven't even reached your first summit and you already see the next six summits that you're going to climb. You want to have your finances totally in order, your relationships and marriage perfect, be in outstanding physical shape, be neat and organized, memorize the Bible and save the world…all this week.

I used to fall into this category. After being in ministry for 13 years and not understanding well this sense of pacing, I burned out. It wasn't just being tired. It wasn't just being weary. It wasn't just a few nights of sleep that weren't sufficient. I had a deep, inner-core burnout. I was at a point where I didn't care about anything or anyone any more. I didn't care anymore what I did for a living. It all just didn't seem to matter.

I was turning into a person that I was unfamiliar with and didn't like. My family was not familiar with this person either, and they didn't like whom I was becoming any more than I did. I felt like my life was out of my control. I needed God's perspective.

Thanks to the input of some godly pastors, parents and friends, and thanks to God for being gracious to speak to me, I was able to turn things around. Since then, I have lived differently than I did the first 13 years in ministry. I stopped going pedal-to-the-metal non-stop all the time. I knew I wanted to be involved in ministry on a long-term basis, and to do that, I needed to pace myself. This was NOT a sprint.

So, I slowed down my pace, evaluated my life and priorities, made the changes I needed to at that time, and started getting back into the race. I made sure I took time for the Lord and for myself. I realized that if I'm not spiritually, emotionally and physically healthy because I've run myself into the ground, I have nothing to offer anyone else. Not my wife, my children, my friends or those at church—no one.

Too Slow?

Some of us, on the other hand, are tempted to go too slowly. We live sluggishly. We don't pray because our knees might hurt. We don't exercise because we might sweat. We don't get on a budget because we wouldn't be able to spend money however we want to. We don't attend church regularly because we can't sleep in. It's all about comfort and ease. It's often true that the slower we go, the more comfortable it is.

However, Hebrews 6 warns us against being sluggish. Verses 11-12 say, "We want each of you to show this same diligence to the end, we do not want you to become lazy." Several verses in Proverbs also tell us not to follow the way of the sluggard. Proverbs 20:4, for example, says, "A sluggard does not plow in season; so at harvest time he looks but finds nothing."

A sense of pace is a hard thing to come by. Often we learn it through trial and error. You don't just discover it overnight. Be patient. Don't be afraid to pick up the pace if you're moving along too slowly and don't be afraid to back off if you feel like you're pressing too much. Again, we need to seek God to show us a proper pace.

God Modeled Pacing

God modeled pacing for us. In Genesis 2:2, we see that God rested on the seventh day. He rested from all His work. It wasn't because God was in Heaven going, "Whew! All this creating has just exhausted me!" No, God was not tired. He could have kept creating galaxies forever.

God rested because He knew He needed to model to humanity a sense of pacing. He said to us, "Six days you will work and on the seventh, you will rest." A day of rest was His idea for us to re-energize ourselves. He showed us that we must balance work with time to rest.

Jesus also had a sense of pace. He gave himself completely in His times of ministry, but He also took time to get away and be with friends and to seek God in prayer. Jesus did not burn out in ministry or constantly live on the ragged edge.

Sometimes slowing yourself down is a matter of making fewer commitments. It's learning to say the two-letter word *No*, along with, *I'm not able to do that.* If we're "man pleasers" we'll be strongly tempted to always say yes to every opportunity that comes our way because we want people to think well of us. Be careful not to do more than the Lord is asking of you. Over-exerting yourself leads to burnout as well as ineffectiveness. Also, run the race set before YOU, not your neighbor. I'm not Frank Shorter. His pace is his and mine is mine—and there is a big difference between the two. Don't try to keep up with others just because you may admire them. Run the wonderful race that the Lord has placed before you, and run it looking only to Him.

Galatians 6:9 says, "Don't grow weary in well doing." This insinuates that you CAN grow weary if you are going at too fast a pace or if you are running in your own power and not the Lord's. When training and running ultra-marathons, I've often thought of Isaiah 40:31: "Yet those who wait for the Lord will gain new strength. They will mount up with wings like eagles, they will run and not get tired, they will walk and not faint."

Knowing when to run, when to walk and when to rest is the key to finishing an ultra-marathon. It's also a key to running the Christian life in a steady and wise manner.

Review:

Principle # 1 – You Must Have a Plan
Principle #2 – YOU MUST HAVE A SENSE OF PACE

It's hard to describe what it's like to be in the middle of 1,500 triathletes who are all starting a 2.4-mile swim bunched together in a rather small starting area. What words come to mind? Hmmm...Dangerous? Hazardous? Treacherous? CRAZY??? Maybe they all apply, but one thing you must remember is to swim defensively. It's easy to get kicked in the face or get hit with an elbow or hand, or, worse yet, have someone swim right over the top of you, pushing you under. Triathletes have been known to come out of the swim with bumps and bruises on their face, goggles knocked off, or, in one case, a broken jaw. Now, this doesn't happen to most, but you must be careful the first 10-15 minutes until everyone spreads out somewhat.

The fastest pros will be out of the water in 45-50 minutes. My goal was one hour and 15 minutes. When you're swimming, 2.4 miles is a long way, and you certainly don't want to go off course and swim any extra distance, which is just what I did. When I got to the turn-around point I realized I was about 100 yards to the *left* of where we were to turn *right* and go around the boat that marked the halfway point. *Oh, well. What's another minute or two in such a long race anyway?* I thought. I looked up at the big digital clock on the boat. 37:00 is what it read.

The hardest part of the swim was the stretch after the turnaround. After you've rounded the boat and started back, it seems like you swim and swim and swim and the shore doesn't get any closer. This was mentally the toughest time in the water. "Stroke, stroke, stroke," I told myself. "I MUST be moving. I MUST be getting closer." But it didn't seem like it. Then, when I could see the shore more clearly and thought I must certainly be almost done, I swam and swam, realizing that I'd misjudged again and wasn't as close as I'd thought. It's very mental.

Finally, I swam through a narrow opening that led to the carpet-covered exit ramp. It sure felt good to have something solid under my feet. There, the NBC cameraman was shooting footage for the two-hour special that would be aired a couple of months later. Ninety-nine percent of what they shoot gets edited out, and my race was part of the edit. One hour and 16 minutes of swimming. "Thank you, Lord, that that is over."

Now, onto the bike. I love to ride and was looking forward to seeing the Hawaiian coastline. I really didn't have any idea what was waiting for me just a few miles down the road.

CHAPTER FOUR
You Must Hydrate and Eat

"Blessed are those who hunger and thirst after righteousness..."
– Matthew 5:6

In the first marathon I ever attempted in 1979, I didn't know anything about the importance of hydration and nutrition in a race. At the time, I was a 10K runner who just drank water whenever I felt thirsty.

The day of the marathon, the temperature soared to more than 100 degrees. At 6 a.m., before the sun had even come up, it was already 80 degrees with 80 percent humidity. I was in for trouble.

I began the race. With each mile marker I passed, I just kept running. I didn't stop to drink or eat. I didn't carry water with me. I hadn't had anything to drink since I started the race, but I kept on running. The first five miles weren't bad, and the next five were okay. At about mile 15 or 16, though, I was feeling badly. By mile 18, I was history. I was completely dehydrated, sick and could no longer run the race. I remained sick for about three days and didn't run again for several months.

I learned the hard way that in any long-distance event, you have to be hydrating and eating throughout the race. If you wait until you're thirsty, it's too late. When I ran the Palo Duro 50-mile race, I carried water with me while I ran and I drank it within the first few miles. Then I stopped at every aid station throughout the race and ate peanut butter and jelly sandwiches and boiled potatoes with salt, and I drank both water and Gatorade. Then I refilled my bottle and got going again. I also carried with me Power Bars and GU packs (GU is a high-carbohydrate concentrated gel. It is not solid, it is not liquid; it is GU).

This 50-mile run had an aid station every three miles, and I stopped at each one to eat and drink, so it was not unlikely that I consumed three to four gallons of fluid during the race. This sounds like an extraordinary amount, but it's what is needed to succeed in an ultra-distance event.

Drink, Drink, Drink

Once, when I was in Florida on vacation, as I was riding my bike in preparation for a 70-mile triathlon in Panama City Beach, I met a fellow pastor named Bob, who was also preparing for the race. He had done several full Ironman triathlons, so I asked him, "What's the secret? If you could pick one thing that's key, what would it be?" He said, "Drink!" He said to start drinking large amounts of water two days before the race. "Force it," he said. "Drink, drink and drink some more." Bob explained how you can actually increase the water volume in your blood if you force fluids over a two-day period.

Our bodies are nearly 70 percent water. Every cell in

every organ contains water. In fact, our brains are about 80 percent water. Our organs need water to function. That is why everyone should drink at least eight glasses of water a day no matter what their activity level.

The average person loses about 2.5 percent of total body water per day. When the loss of water through perspiration is greatly increased, but the intake of water is not, dehydration may result in serious physical problems within a few hours. As dehydration progresses, the tissues tend to shrink because they are losing water. This is why a lack of water causes our muscles to weaken, our blood to thicken and our heart rates to elevate.

Not getting enough water into our bodies, especially when we undergo long-distance endeavors, can take us out of the race and even be life-threatening. This is true in our spiritual lives as well.

Spiritual Hydration

In our Christian walk, we need to "drink, drink and drink some more," as Bob said. Being spiritually hydrated is the most important key to spiritual endurance. We need to drink deeply and regularly of the Holy Spirit and nourish ourselves with the truth of God's Word. We must spend time thinking about and talking to Jesus, meditating on scripture, worshipping and praising God, praying, and staying full of the Holy Spirit. It is letting God's life rise up in us so that we have His strength to do all the things He is asking us to do. We do this so that we can make it to the end of the race. So that we can endure.

Jesus is described in the Bible as the "Living Water" and the "Bread of Life." Water is a very important concept in scripture.

- John 4:14–"The water that I give him will be in him, springs of water, welling up to eternal life."
- Isaiah 43:20–"I give water in the wilderness, rivers in the desert, to give drink to my chosen people."
- John 7:38–"He who believes in me, out of his heart shall flow rivers of living water."
- Revelation 7:17–"For the lamb in the midst of the throne will be their Shepherd and He will guide them to springs of living water."
- Revelation 22:1–"Then He showed me the river of the water of life, flowing from the throne of God and the Lamb."
- Revelation 22:17–"The Spirit and the bride say, 'Come!' Let him who is thirsty come. Let him who desires to take the water of life come."

The man that I mentioned in Chapter 1 who hiked solo across Antarctica paid heed to the importance of hydration and eating. He knew that he would be losing 45 pounds during his journey. So in preparation for his trek, he ate six tablespoons of olive oil and more than a stick of butter each day.

That doesn't sound very appetizing, does it? Matthew 5:6 says, "Blessed are those who hunger and thirst after righteousness, for they shall by filled (hydrated)." We must take in the Power Bar of the Bible, the GU pack of the Holy Ghost, the Gatorade of God's life, and the living water of Jesus on a regular basis. Hydrating and feasting on Jesus will keep our spirits refreshed and our spiritual muscles strong.

Take a look at a piece of beef jerky. Dry, shriveled, hard– basically pretty ugly. Put that same piece of beef jerky in a bowl of water overnight and notice the difference the next morning. It will be hydrated, flexible and soft. Which picture best mirrors our spiritual muscles? Are we spiritually shriveled and dry? Or are we well hydrated and nourished spiritually? We must be if we're ever going to see the finish line.

Review:

Principle # 1 – You Must Have a Plan
Principle # 2 – You Must Have a Sense of Pace
Principle # 3 – YOU MUST HYDRATE AND EAT

After a quick stop in the changing tent to get my cycling clothes on, I found my bike and was off, riding through hundreds of spectators, including Jennifer and several other friends of ours who were there. The bike route headed up a very steep hill then turned left out onto the Queen K Highway. I knew how important it was to take in lots of calories during the bike leg, so I immediately downed a peanut butter and jelly sandwich that I had taped to my bike. I scarfed that thing, eating the whole sandwich in about three bites for some reason. Why? Who knows? Excitement perhaps. One should only start eating after about 20 minutes on the bike and then slowly nibble. I made a big mistake. From that point on I didn't feel good for many hours. The sandwich just sat in my stomach. But, that was the least of the concerns I would have.

The first 20 miles of biking went well, other than my stomach. I was riding in pretty good weather conditions along the Pacific Ocean when the reality of the Hawaiian Ironman hit home…hard and fast. Out of nowhere the winds hit head on with a force that felt like a runaway 18-wheeler. My speed on the bike dropped from 18-20 mph to about 8 mph. I'd never faced winds like this in all my life. As if 112 miles are not far enough, going into winds of 40-50 mph made this race begin to seem impossible to finish. I couldn't push too hard through the wind for fear that my thigh muscle would get re-injured, seize up and end my race. Aid stations that were set up along the bike route were literally blowing away. Three riders were actually blown right off their bikes. After more than an hour of facing ferocious winds, and considering the huge number of miles yet to cover, I hit emotional rock bottom. As I tried to press on, my eyes filled with tears.

Discouraging thoughts clouded my mind. *This is a once in a lifetime opportunity and I'm not going to be able to do it. I can't believe this.* I'd never quit anything in my life, but I began to realize that this race can melt the resolve of even the most resolute.

CHAPTER FIVE

You Must Protect Your Feet

"…forbearing one another…forgiving each other…"
– Colossians 3:13

In a triathlon a few years ago, we all began by swimming in the Gulf of Mexico. After I came out the water, I ran across the sand and onto the parking lot where the bikes were. I had prepared a tub of water to step into so that I could get the rocks and sand off my feet, and then I was going to step onto a towel. After that I was going to put on my socks and bike shoes and be off again.

I stood on my towel and wiped my feet a bit and started putting on my socks, when I realized I hadn't stepped into the tub. I thought, "It's okay. It won't matter that much." So I finished pulling on my socks and shoes, hopped onto my bike and biked the 56 miles. No problem.

Then it came time to switch to running. I transferred from my biking shoes to my running shoes and took off. About a mile and a half into the run, I felt a burning sensation on the ball of my left foot. It was friction. I figured I could endure a little pain and make it the 13 miles, so I didn't do anything.

By the third mile, however, my foot was screaming in pain. I finally stopped, took off my shoe and got the piece of gravel out. A pebble from the sand after the swim, so many miles before, had given me a blister. I lubricated it with Vaseline and then began running again. I had to stop five more times to tend to that blister. It cost me probably five to seven minutes in the race. In these types of events, you have to guard against friction.

Friction generates heat. When that heat gets to a certain point, our bodies release water to that spot under our skin. The result is a blister. If the friction continues, the blister can break open and the situation can get ugly and serious very quickly. Participating in ultra-marathons and watching endurance events on television, I've seen some very ugly feet that have been torn to ribbons because of friction that wasn't dealt with. I've had blisters the size of sliver dollars on the bottom of my feet due to these races. I once lost seven toenails after one race due to the rubbing and friction against my shoes. Ouch! I did a very poor job in that race of caring for my feet (OK, call me Captain Obvious for that last statement).

Spiritual Protection

Protecting our feet in the spiritual realm is also of utmost importance. Most of the things that cause friction and blisters in our lives are relational in nature. If you're married, have children, work with others, have parents, siblings, friends or neighbors (which we all do), you know that friction can, and probably will, be something you have to deal with in these relationships. Each person you interact with represents a potential point of friction.

It can take only one pebble to knock you out of a race. Likewise, one very small, seemingly insignificant pebble in your relational shoe can rub you and disrupt you, and if you don't confront it early on, cause a blister. Satan can use it and blow it completely out of proportion. You can find yourself wiped right off the mountain. You can be taken out of the race because of one little pebble.

Over the years, I've learned more about protecting feet when running. I have learned about the Spiro Flex blister dressings. It's something you put on before you get blisters. It's sort of like a second skin. I also have learned that before the race starts, it's helpful to put petroleum jelly all over the feet. There are also running "gaiters" made of cloth and elastic that you can strap around your ankles and the top of your shoes to keep pebbles and stones out during long races on dirt trails.

How Do We Protect Our Spiritual Feet?

If we want to prevent relational friction from turning into ugly, relational blisters, we need to address what caused the friction. We have to learn to forgive and keep short accounts with people. We have to walk in brokenness before one another. We need to learn to say "I'm sorry. I was wrong. Will you forgive me?" These are perhaps the most powerful nine words in any language.

Do you remember the TV show *Happy Days*? Remember how the always cool Fonzie could never say he was wrong? The word "wrong" would get stuck in his mouth when he tried to say it. He'd say, "I was wwwr...I was wwwrr..." He couldn't get the word out because of pride.

We need to swallow our pride. Better yet, we need to repent of pride. We need to communicate when there's a problem, and we need to be open to hearing about our mistakes from others. God's word says, "Faithful are the wounds of a friend." (Proverbs 27:6)

Managing Conflict

Conflict in relationships is guaranteed. Friction is guaranteed. Problems are guaranteed. Just as there is no way you're going to participate in any distance event and not have some kind of friction, there is no way you'll have a friction-free life with friction-free relationships. The key is in how we handle it and what we do with it.

What do you do with the friction in your life? Do you lubricate it with forgiveness? Do you apply an attitude of brokenness to blisters? Do you wear the gaiters of Godliness to keep out the pebbles of pride that try to sneak in? Do you respond to situations out of God's love? If you do, you have just increased the odds of reaching the finish line.

If you have a plan and a sense of pace, if you hydrate and nourish yourself spiritually, and you protect your feet by learning to live in harmony with other people, you are well on your way!

Review:

Principle # 1 – You Must Have a Plan
Principle # 2 – You Must Have a Sense of Pace
Principle # 3 – You Must Hydrate and Eat
Principle # 4 – YOU MUST PROTECT YOUR FEET (RELATIONSHIPS)

"For You are high and lifted up, the glory of the nations, You are high and lifted up, the Lord of all the Earth…" A simple worship chorus began to play over and over in my mind. It started to lift my spirits as I pressed through the howling winds. I began to think of my family and different friends who I knew were praying for me that day. I thought about the amazing way the Lord had gotten me into this race and what His purposes were in my being there, THAT year, in THAT Ironman race. Was it all to stop because the going was tough...REALLY tough? I prayed that the joy of the Lord would be my strength. I thanked the Lord for each rotation of the peddles on my bike. I began to actually sing out loud. Maybe there was still a flame of hope flickering. By God's grace and strength, maybe I could finish.

After riding for about 40 miles, the bike course starts a stair-step climb up a volcano. The climb went on for many miles, and the winds came crashing down on all of us as we tried to push up the hill. Going *uphill* into winds of this magnitude made for the toughest cycling miles I've ever ridden. Finally, when I arrived at Hawi, the small Hawaiian town that marked the bike turn-around point, I was physically wasted. My gas tank was reading "E" and there were no gas stations in sight.

I grabbed my halfway bag with food and drink in it. All the athletes turn these in at the beginning of the day and the bags are driven up to Hawi. The triathletes grab them when they arrive there. I decided to do something I had not planned on. I took my bag, pulled over to the side of the road, got off my bike and sat down in the grass. As I sat there, I watched rider after rider go past me and head down the hill. I was completely exhausted from fighting the terrible winds, yet had about 60 miles to bike and a 26.2-mile marathon to run after that. As I sat there, again, I began to doubt.

CHAPTER SIX
Learn to Handle Pain, Setbacks and Failure

"Blessed is the man who endures painful trials…" – *James 1:12*

We all have to learn to handle pain, setbacks and failure. This is at the heart of endurance, isn't it? You have to learn to handle these because if there's not some pain, some setbacks and some failures, the word endurance really doesn't apply. For example, when I'm home lying on the couch with my chips, watching my favorite team on the tube, endurance really doesn't apply to that situation, does it? I'm not enduring anything, except perhaps a poor showing from my team. When you think of endurance you don't picture yourself lying on a float in a swimming pool with a Coke in your hand.

So when we think about these three things—pain, setbacks, and failure–they really get to the heart of what we're talking about. In any type of sporting event there is going to be some kind of pain guaranteed, but you have to learn to manage it, deal with it and even, at times, fight through it.

In sports there are some tricks of the trade to manage and keep pain minimal. Ibuprofen and Excedrin, for example, can relieve the pain you feel. Some coaches say not to do this because you need to have an accurate read-out of your body. If you've hurt yourself, you need to know it. But every now and then I have been known to use these painkillers because they really do help.

In the same way, spiritually, you need to find out what the pain relievers are for you. When you're in pain and really hurting inside, seek the Lord and He'll show you what relieves pain for you. I don't know what works for you, but if you're in pain, ask the Lord, "Lord, what are two or three things that would serve as pain relievers for me?" It may be music, spending time with a trusted friend, a book, a weekend away, journaling...who knows? Find what it is and take it as a gift from the Lord.

Friendly with Pain?

Still, we have to learn to manage the pain we feel. We have to become friendly with it, since it's unavoidable. We need to learn to love, trust and depend upon the Lord throughout the painful time.

In our society we are so adverse to pain. It started when we were little...very little. Just being born is very painful. Have you ever seen a newborn baby come out smiling or laughing? I haven't. They usually are screaming their heads off. As soon as my son, Kyle, was born, they immediately poked his heel with a razor type instrument to draw blood, slapped him, then they wrapped him up like a mummy so he couldn't move. That's a painful way to start life.

How many of you were scared to death to go to the doctor and get a shot when you were little? Or how about getting a loose tooth pulled out by your Dad or having your Mom dig out a splinter? All were traumatic because of one thing—pain.

In sporting events, I've experienced all kinds of pain—pulled muscles, blisters, dehydration, intestinal cramping, sore knees, extreme weariness, even stinging nettles, which are plants with acid on the leaves…

Once, when I was running a half marathon, I had to hop off the road for a moment because I had applied the hydration principle very well. After I came back up and out of the grove of trees and started running again, I noticed that my legs were starting to burn. I thought, *This is weird!* After a few more steps, it felt like they were on fire. I looked down and I had red marks all over my legs. It looked like I'd been whipped with a lash. I had been in a patch of stinging nettles. Ouch!

The last three miles of that race, my legs were on fire. Talk about pain. But what are you going to do, stop in the middle of the race? No. You have to keep on going. Life is full of pain. And we need to learn how to deal with it.

James gives us some perspective. James 1:2 says, "Count it all joy when you meet painful trials…" James 1:12 tells us, "Blessed is the man who endures painful trials..." So there's a perspective on pain that is biblical. It's a godly perspective that we can have as we go through painful times and events. By God's grace and through His strength we can count it joy when we suffer pain.

II Timothy 3:12 instructs, "All who desire to live a godly life will be persecuted." Persecution often means pain. So all who desire to live a godly life will experience pain. Sometimes the internal pain of hurt emotions is worse than physical pain. Usually this comes from another person, and often, fellow Christians. With wise counsel and a right heart, pain can be dealt with over time. Quite often forgiveness seems to be a key in seeing pain slowly alleviated. God can heal hurting hearts and emotions.

Setbacks

What are setbacks? Setbacks are those things out of your control that go wrong. How do you handle those things?

I was in a triathlon in Kansas City a few years ago, and the man who was winning was a professional triathlete. He was just flying on the bike. It was an 18-mile bike loop, and at 10 miles, his back tire went flat. So he had a choice to make. He could either stop and fix the tire, which would put him out of the race–meaning giving up his chance to win or he could keep going. He kept going. He biked the last eight miles on his back rim. He went much more slowly after that because he didn't have an inflated tire. The second-place rider passed him, then the third-place rider. But he kept going anyway. After the bike portion of the race came the run. When he started into the run, he was in third place. But he passed the other two guys and won the race. He overcame the setback.

Hoops

Due to seven players fouling out—a definite setback— North Jackson High School basketball team in Stevenson, Ala., was down to two players, both of them playing with four fouls. So there were two players against five on the floor for Fort Payne High School. There was a minute left in overtime and North Jackson's two-man team was behind by five points. The two-man team came down the court, launched a three-pointer and made it, closing the gap to only two points. Fort Payne dribbled up court, missed a shot and the ball went out of bounds.

Robert Collier of North Jackson inbounded the ball to Chad Cobb, who was fouled. He went to the line. His first free throw went in, as did the second. The game was now tied. Fort Payne took possession of the ball, but turned it over again on a traveling call with 13 seconds left. After a timeout, Collier had to inbound the ball to Cobb. One player guarded Collier on the inbound pass, and three guarded Cobb, but Cobb eluded all three defenders along the baseline and took the pass. Cobb dribbled the length of the floor and missed what seemed to be the final desperation shot. But Collier rebounded and put the ball back in the basket to seal a truly amazing comeback.

Two men against five. They didn't give up. They endured and won the game.

How do you handle the setbacks in your life? If you're going to make it to the finish line, you've got to be able to handle setbacks and not let them take you out of the game or race.

Abraham Lincoln

Probably the greatest example of handling setbacks well is Abraham Lincoln. If you want to learn about somebody who didn't quit, look no further. Born into poverty, Lincoln was faced with pain, setbacks and failure throughout his life. His brother Thomas died in infancy, his mother died when he was 9 years old, and then his sister died 10 years later. Later the woman believed to be his first fiancé died before they could marry. He twice failed in business and was in debt; he suffered from severe depression; and in politics, he won several state and national elections, but also lost several before becoming the 16th President of the United States.

He could have quit many times—but he didn't; and because he didn't quit, he became one of the greatest Presidents in the history of our country. Lincoln was a champion and he never gave up. Here is a sketch of Lincoln's road to the White House:

- 1832 – He runs for Illinois state legislature and loses. Also this year he loses his job.
- 1833 – He borrows some money to open a store and it fails; he is severely in debt.
- 1834 – He runs for state legislature and wins.
- 1835 – He is engaged to be married but his fiancé dies.
- 1836 – He receives his law license and is re-elected to the state legislature. Later he suffers from severe depression.
- 1837 – He proposes to Mary Owens and is turned down; their courtship ends.
- 1838 – He is re-elected to the state legislature and seeks to become speaker of the state legislature but is defeated.
- 1840 – He is re-elected to the state legislature and again tries for speaker of the state legislature but is defeated. He argues his first case against the Illinois Supreme Court. He becomes engaged to Mary Todd.
- 1841 – He breaks off his engagement with Mary Todd and suffers from depression.
- 1842 – He resumes his courtship with Mary Todd and they marry. (Later they have four children.)
- 1843 – He runs for Congress and loses.
- 1846 – He runs for Congress again and wins.
- 1850 – His son Edward dies.
- 1854 – He runs for U.S. Senate and loses.
- 1856 – He seeks the vice-presidential nomination for the Republican Party but loses.
- 1858 – He runs for the U.S. Senate again and loses. He makes his famous "House Divided" speech.
- 1860 – He is elected President of the United States.

Failure

What about failure? I know we've all experienced times when we feel like we're the king or queen of failure. But the true measure of our character is not whether we fail or not (because we all do), but in what we do with our failures.

How do you handle your failures? How have other people handled theirs?

Did you know that a newspaper editor fired Walt Disney for a lack of ideas? True. Also, both Walt Disney and Henry Ford went broke four or five times before they finally succeeded with their business ideas. Thomas Edison tried several hundred times to create the light bulb but failed every time. Finally, after hundreds of attempts that did not work, he discovered the answer to his problem. I'm sure glad he didn't give up after all his failures.

And what about Peter? He denied the Lord three times. And looking at the Old Testament, what of Jonah who ran away from God, and David who committed adultery and murder? Talk about failures. Kings Saul and Solomon had failure as part of their life stories, too. Abraham lied to protect his own skin. Jacob deceived to get an inheritance meant for his older brother.

Sometimes in this area of pain, setbacks and failures, our greatest enemy is ourselves. We're hard on ourselves. And sometimes we're our greatest enemy. It's like the sign in the office that said, "If you could kick the person most responsible for your problems, YOU wouldn't be able to sit down for a week."

At many points the diary of Christopher Columbus you will find this quote: "This day we sailed on."

This day we sailed on. No mention of the storms, the *Piñto* breaking apart. No mention of the hunger, the disease or the sailors who died. Simply, "This day we sailed on." That could be a great motto for Christians. This day we sailed on.

Here's a poem that summarizes this principle of pain, set-backs and failure:

THE RACE
By D.H. Groberg

A children's race—young boys, young men
How I remember well.
Excitement, sure! But also fear;
It wasn't hard to tell.

They all lined up so full of hope;
Each thought to win the race.
Or tie for first, or if not that,
At least take second place.

And fathers watched from off the side.
Each cheering for his son.
And each boy hoped to show his dad
That he would be the one.

The whistle blew and off they went!
Young hearts and hopes afire.
To win and be the hero there
Was each young boy's desire.

And one boy in particular
Whose dad was in the crowd,
Was running near the lead and thought,
"My dad will be so proud!"

But as they speeded down the field
Across a shallow dip,
The little boy who thought to win
Lost his step and slipped.

Trying hard to catch himself
His hands flew out to brace,
And mid the laughter of the crowd
He fell flat on his face.

So down he fell and with him hope
He couldn't win it now.
Embarrassed, sad, he only wished
To disappear somehow.

But as he fell his dad stood up
And showed his anxious face,
Which to the boy so clearly said:
"Get up and win the race."

He quickly rose, no damage done.
Behind a bit, That's all.
And ran with all his mind and might
To make up for that fall.

So anxious to restore himself
To catch up and to win.
His mind went faster than his legs:
He slipped and fell again.

He wished then he had quit before
With only one disgrace.
"I'm hopeless as a runner now;
I shouldn't try to race."

And in the laughing crowd he searched
And found his father's face.
That steady look which said again:
"Get up and win the race!"

So up he jumped to try again
Ten yards behind the last,
"If I'm to gain those yards," he thought,
"I've got to move real fast."

Exerting everything he had
He gained eight or ten.
But trying so hard to catch the lead
He slipped and fell again!

Defeat! He lay there silently,
A tear dropped from his eye.
"There's no sense running anymore;
Three strikes: I'm out! Why try?"

The will to rise had disappeared,
All hope had fell away.
So far behind, so error prone:
A loser all the way.

"I've lost, so what's the use," he thought.
"I'll live with my disgrace."
But then he thought about his dad,
Who soon he'd have to face.

"Get up." An echo sounded low.
"Get up and take your place;
You were not meant for failure here.
Get up and win the race."

"With borrowed will, get up," it said.
"You haven't lost at all,
For winning is no more than this:
To rise each time you fall."

So up he rose to run once more,
and with a new commit
He resolved that win or lose
At least he wouldn't quit.

So far behind the others now,
The most he'd ever been.
Still he gave it all he had
And ran as though to win.

Three times he'd fallen, stumbling,
Three times he rose again;
Too far behind to hope to win
He still ran to the end.

They cheered the winning runner
As he crossed the line first place.
Head high, and proud, and happy;
No falling, no disgrace.

But when the fallen youngster
Crossed the line last place,
The crowd gave him the greater cheer

For finishing the race.

And even though he came in last
With head bowed low, unproud.
You would have thought he won the race
To listen to the crowd.

And to his dad he sadly said,
"I didn't do so well."
"To me you won," his father said.
"You rose each time you fell."

And now when things seem dark and hard
And difficult to face,
The memory of that little boy
Helps me in my race.

For all of life is like that race.
With ups and downs and all.
And all you have to do to win,
Is rise each time you fall.

"Quit! Give up! You're beaten!"
They still shout in my face.
But another voice within me says:
"GET UP AND WIN THE RACE!"

How do you handle pain, setbacks, and failure? Let's learn
to trust in the Lord and rest in His great care for us. Let's get
up each time we fall and keep pressing on. Proverbs 24:16
says, "A righteous man falls seven times, and rises again." I
love that verse. It does not matter how many times I fall. I'm
getting back up every time.

Jesus faced more pain and setbacks than any other person
who ever lived. He overcame them all. If we are followers of
Christ, He lives in us and can overcome again through us if
we'll abide in His great life within.

Review:

Principle # 1 – You Must Have a Plan
Principle # 2 – You Must Have a Sense of Pace
Principle # 3 – You Must Hydrate And Eat
Principle # 4 – You Must Protect Your Feet (Relationships)
Principle # 5 – LEARN TO HANDLE PAIN, SETBACKS AND FAILURE

I ate my food, got up off the grass, replaced empty water bottles with full ones, got on my bike, and, feeling like I was about in 1499th place out of the 1,500 competitors, started riding down the mountain. Now I faced a new challenge. The strong winds were at my back and I was flying down the mountain. Good news you'd think; however, the danger of crashing skyrocketed as the speed increased. The road began to curve to the left causing the tailwinds to become cross-winds. I clung to the handlebars remembering reports of those who, in previous years, had been blown off their bikes by the winds blasting them from the side at this point in the race. With white knuckles I hung on and flew down the mountain seeking that balance of speed and safety. The next long portion of the bike leg saw the winds shifting depending on where I was on the course. These winds shifted all during the day so at times they helped and other times proved to be a cruel enemy.

At about 85 miles I began to get nauseated. I had attempted to eat and drink regularly during the entire ride to get the nourishment necessary for this type of race. However, something was going wrong. The further I pressed on, the sicker I began to feel. Finally, I rode by the airport, then the Natural Energy Lab. These were key markers letting me know that I was getting close to the town of Kona again. I really started to believe that if I could just get off my bike I might finish. As I approached Kona on my bike, I began to pass the pro men who were FINISHING their race. That's right. I actually heard the loud speaker a few blocks from where I was riding announcing that Peter Reid from Canada was coming down the home stretch to the finish line. Wow. Reid was finishing the race while I still had eight miles yet to bike and then a marathon to run. Depressing! I rode through town toward the bike-to-run transition, exhausted and nauseated, but excited to see Jen and my other friends, who I just knew would be there waiting for me with some much needed love and encouragement. I was, however, one and one half hours behind the schedule I had been hoping for.

CHAPTER SEVEN
You Must Develop a No-Limits Mentality

"He is able to do far more, exceedingly, abundantly, above all we could ask or think..." – *Ephesians 3:20*

There's a quote I once read about the Ironman Triathalon. It went like this:

> *The Ironman Triathalon is a contest conjured by someone without a sense of limits. Mankind has been extremely competent at imposing restrictions upon himself, his mind, and his body. The Ironman is a means of removing those restrictions so that what once was thought impossible becomes possible. Men and women operate on a day-to-day level of about 10-15 percent. What a race like this does is show you what 100 percent is.*

My experience in ultra-endurance events has shown me that I can do much, much more than I ever thought I could. I remember the first 10K race I was in. It seemed so far. I think the farthest I had run before that was three or four miles, so to go 6.2, well, that seemed like a very long way.

But I entered, and when I crossed the finish line, a mental limitation barrier suddenly came down. Next, I tried a half-marathon—13 miles. I finished, and another mental limitation came down. Then I attempted a marathon and finished. Another limitation came down. After that, I signed up for a 50-mile race and finished. Again, limitations crumbled.

Do you see what was happening? A much larger percentage of this is mental than most people realize. Most of you reading this book could finish a marathon. Maybe you wouldn't run the entire way, but you could probably finish.

Some of you are thinking, "No way! That would be impossible!" It's only impossible because you think it is, not because it actually is. I'm not trying to get you to run a marathon. I'm just saying that if you would get past the mental barriers that you have established in your head, you would be amazed at what you could do.

Think of all the things you have done in your life that you once thought were impossible, but now you realize they're not because you've done them. You probably could come up with a list of several things in this category.

Growing up, I never thought I could give anyone a shot. I mean really, sticking a sharp metal object into someone's body? I couldn't do it. But then my wife, Jennifer, had a high-risk pregnancy, and I had to give her a shot twice a week. I *had* to learn how. The doctor told me to practice on an orange. The day came when I had to give Jennifer her first injection. I was sure that I'd stick her so hard that the only thing left sticking out would be the little nub you press your thumb on. Or, I feared that I'd be too soft, and trying to be gentle, have the needle barely go in. Then, of course I'd have to push it in hard the rest of the way. But she was kind and gracious to me, and I was able to give her the shots—they were especially handy in the middle of any disagreement. "Time for your shot, dear!"

The Tarahumara Indians of Copper Canyon in Northwestern Mexico seem to grow up without a sense of limits when it comes to running long distances. From youth to adulthood, they watch and participate in long distance running. They have been called the greatest endurance runners in the world. They have been known to run 200 miles over a period of three days and nights. One of the methods they use to hunt deer is to chase the animal until it drops from exhaustion. Rabbits and turkeys are also hunted in the same manner.

These people have no mental boundaries imposed on them as they grow up when it comes to covering massive distances on foot. Running for hours on end is normal and natural to them, and, the longer the better. Once, when given an important message to deliver, one Tarahumara man ran nearly 600 miles in five days to see it delivered. This was over rough terrain at high altitude. When it comes to running, the Tarahumara people have no limitations in their minds.

A No-Limits God

God says that all things are possible with Him. See Jeremiah 32:17 and Mark 10:27. What is this God that lives inside of us capable of? Ephesians 3:20, "He, (God) is able to do far more, exceedingly, abundantly above all we could ask or think..."

These are no-limits verses because we have a no-limits God. There are no limits to His grace and there are no limits to His patience. There are no limits to His favor upon us or His love for us. There is no limit to any of His great attributes.

The Bible is full of no-limits people. Joseph was in a pit

and then later in a dungeon. Those are places of limitation, and yet he became the number-two ruler in all of Egypt.

David, the lowly shepherd boy, though limited in his military experience and limited in his governing experience, defeated Goliath and became king of Israel.

Peter, limited with the knowledge that says "human beings weigh too much to walk on water," by faith, got out of the boat and walked on water toward Jesus. Moses at the Red Sea, limited by lots of water in front of him, the Egyptian army behind him and mountains on either side, raised his rod and suddenly there was a way out.

Esther, limited by a law that said, "You can't just go in to the king anytime you want," boldly went in anyway, setting the limitations aside, and saved the nation of Israel.

Jesus—who was nailed to a bloody cross and put in a tomb so that all hell said, "There! We finally limited Him!"—rose again! He rose up as reigning King, unlimited in power, unlimited in glory, unlimited in majesty, unlimited in splendor, in knowledge and wisdom. And he lives in every believer by His unlimited Spirit.

Our flesh encourages us to live in the comfort zone, but God is calling us to live in the no-limits zone. We shouldn't say, "*I can't.*" We should remember scripture and say, "I can do all things through Christ who strengthens me" (Philippians 4:13).

Others Can Hold Us Back

Sometimes we face limitations that come from the words of others:

"You'll never amount to anything."

"You could never do that."

"You want to do what? Ha!"

Thomas Edison's teacher said he was too stupid to learn anything. Albert Einstein's teacher described him as mentally slow. And Beethoven's music teacher described him hopeless as a composer. They all missed it a little bit, wouldn't you say? Aren't we glad they didn't listen to those naysayers?

Once there was a little country schoolhouse that was heated by an old-fashioned, pot-bellied coal stove. A little boy had the job of coming to school early each day to start the fire and warm the room before his teacher and his classmates arrived.

One morning the teacher and students arrived to find the schoolhouse engulfed in flames. They dragged the unconscious little boy out of the flaming building more dead than alive. He had major burns over the lower half of his body and was taken to the nearby county hospital.

From his bed the dreadfully burned, semiconscious little boy faintly heard the doctor talking to his mother. The doctor told his mother that her son would surely die, which was for the best, really, he said, because the terrible fire had devastated the lower half of his body.

But the brave boy didn't want to die. He made up his mind that he would survive. Somehow, to the amazement of the physician, he did survive. When the mortal danger was past, he again heard the doctor and his mother speaking quietly. The mother was told that since the fire had destroyed so much flesh in the lower part of his body, it would almost be better if he had died, since he was doomed to be a lifetime cripple with no use at all of his lower limbs.

Once more the brave boy made up his mind. He would not be a cripple. He would walk. But unfortunately, from the waist down, he had no motor ability. His thin legs just dangled there, all but lifeless.

After he was released from the hospital, his mother would

massage his little legs every day. But there was no feeling, no control, nothing. Still, his determination that he would walk was as strong as ever.

When he wasn't in bed, he was confined to a wheelchair. One sunny day his mother wheeled him out into the yard to get some fresh air. This day, instead of sitting there, he threw himself from the chair and pulled himself along the grass, dragging his legs behind him. He worked his way to the white-picket fence bordering their lot. And with great effort, he raised himself up on the fence, and then stake by stake began dragging himself along the fence, resolved that he would walk.

He started to do this every day, until he wore a smooth path all around the yard beside the fence. There was nothing he wanted more than to develop life in those legs. Ultimately through daily massages, his iron persistence and his amazing determination, he developed the ability to stand up and to walk haltingly. Then he learned to walk by himself.

He began to walk to school, and then he began to run to school for the sheer joy of running. Later in college, he made the track team. Still later, in Madison Square Garden, this young man who was not expected to survive, who would surely never walk, who could never hope to run, this determined young man, Dr. Glen Cunningham, set a world track record in the mile. He didn't let others' opinions keep him from his goal. He's a no-limits man.

Racing with No Legs

I was getting ready to compete in a 70-mile triathlon a few years ago and was down on the beach, waiting for the race to start. Before we got into the Gulf of Mexico for the swimming portion of the race, I was startled when I turned to my right and saw a man coming toward the water with no legs. He was propelling himself forward on only his hands; fully prepared with his goggles, swim cap and wetsuit. I saw him throw himself into the water and start to swim. I thought, "There goes a no-limits person right there."

We need no-limits people in the kingdom of God. There was a survey done on 100-year-olds that asked them, "If you could do anything different in life, what would you do?" One of the answers that kept coming up was, "I would have taken more risks."

We need to take risks for God's glory. We need to pull down mental barriers. If we're going to reach the finish line of what God has in store for us, we have to develop a no-limits, faith-filled heart and outlook.

A No-Limits Power Source

Have you ever picked up a flashlight and tried to switch it on, only to discover it was hollow? No batteries. No power source. The power sources in long-distance endurance races are fit muscles, proper nutrition and fluid intake, mental toughness, good encouragement, etc. What about the Christian race? We must understand the connection we have with our spiritual power source. The very life of God is that source. It's His divine life, which is so far above and beyond human life that it's difficult to comprehend. God's life is complete. God lacks nothing. He has no needs. He created us. We have needs. He alone can fulfill those needs. How does He do that? If He is our power source, how do we, as those who have submitted to Christ's rule in our lives, connect with that source of life?

We need to understand that the power source resides within us. Look at the following verses (italics added):

- I John 4:4, "…greater is He *who lives in you* than he who is in the world"
- Galatians 2:20, "I am crucified with Christ; nevertheless, I live, yet not I but *Christ lives in me…*"
- Colossians 1:27, "…*Christ in you,* the hope of glory."
- I Corinthians 6:16, "Do you not know that your body is the temple (dwelling place) of *the Holy Spirit, who lives within you?*"
- 2 Corinthians 6:16, "I will dwell *in them* and walk *in them* and I will be their God and they will be my people."
- 2 Corinthians 13:5, "…do you not know that *Christ is in you…*"

In John 14:20 Jesus said, "In that day you will know that I am in the Father, and *you in me and I in you.*" Jesus lives in every believer to be their Lord, Savior, and their very *life*…their power source. You see, we were not meant to live the Christian life. Jesus must re-live His divine life through us. Ever try to forgive someone 77 times in a row? Ever try to give your shirt to the person who sued you to get your coat? Ever try to love your enemy? Most of us get very frustrated trying to be "good Christians" because we often discover we just can't do it. Again, we weren't meant to.

Our job is simply to abide in Christ, our life's power source. Let's understand that we cannot live the Christian life, but we can determine whether or not that life is lived through us. John 15 gives us the picture of a branch abiding in a tree (vine). The life giving sap of the tree is the life of the branch. The branch stays alive and bears fruit as the sap flows from the tree into it. John 15:4 says, "Abide in me and I in you. As the branch cannot bear fruit by itself unless it abides in the vine, neither can you unless you abide in me."

Try to run the Christian life on your own power and through your own strength, and you will struggle endlessly. Live in Christ. Let Him live in and flow through you. Abide, remain, in Him. Acknowledge that you cannot live the Christian life, and thank Him that He has provided all you need for this race. Abundantly, without limits.

Remember, the Christian life is not your responsibility but your response, to his ability. Remember too, that every demand placed on you is a demand placed on the life of Christ within you. Good news!

Second Peter 1:3, "…His divine power *has given* unto *us all things* that pertain to *life and godliness* through the knowledge of His Son."

Review:

Principle # 1 - You Must Have a Plan
Principle # 2 - You Must Have a Sense Of Pace
Principle # 3 - You Must Hydrate And Eat
Principle # 4 - You Must Protect Your Feet (Relationships)
Principle # 5 – Learn To Handle Pain, Setbacks And Failure
Principle # 6 – YOU MUST DEVELOP A NO- LIMITS MENTALITY

The last mile of the 112-mile bike leg has a short but very steep hill. It was like someone cruelly put it there just to finish off all those who had made it that far. I saw a triathlete walking his bike up it. *No way*, I thought. I stood up and, mashing on the pedals, slowly inched over the final hill and coasted down to the Kona Surf Resort, looking for Jen. I made it, and my thigh had not blown up. "Thank you Lord!" I didn't see Jen or anyone else I knew as I dismounted my bike. (I

remember thinking, *I'm not getting back on that bike for months!*)
I grabbed my bag with my running gear and sat down in the
changing tent. This was not how you'd want to feel just
before launching into a marathon. Normally, when only running a marathon, I'd rested a good deal the last few days
before the race, backing way off on training so I'd feel strong
on race day. Boy, what a difference today!

I changed and walked out of the tent. I was still quite nauseated besides feeling like someone had hooked up an energy
sucking vacuum cleaner to my body and suctioned out all my
strength. I continued to look for those loved ones who could
encourage me, but they were nowhere to be found. The
encouragement I had hoped to receive and so badly needed
was not there. Where were they?

When you leave the bike-to-run transition area, you
immediately are confronted with, what else, a steep hill, followed by a long downhill run into what is called "The Pit."
What goes down must come up… so the first few miles of the
marathon just seem to add insult to injury. By now, I was
pretty sure I'd be losing my stomach at any time. I was doing
a lot of walking and a little running. There were aid stations
set up every mile or two with the best people in the world
running them. Encouraging words along with refreshments
were freely given out. I received the words, but the thought
of food made me want to hurl.

At about mile six, as I ran along the ocean, which was to
my left, I saw some friends, Bob and Kathy, who lived in
Kona. It was so great to see someone I actually knew. No time
to stop and talk though. Kathy snapped a few photos and
they wished me well as I went by. I remembered being
embarrassed by how late in the day it was and how poorly
my race was going. I started drinking de-fizzed Coke at the
aid stations remembering that it can settle an upset stomach.

Then, from down the road, I heard a booming voice. Someone was shouting at the top of his voice and was running toward me, though still a couple of blocks away. "Go, Linc! You're THE MAN! You look great! You can do it!" It was my upbeat, always positive friend, Todd. Now, I knew I wasn't THE MAN, and that I didn't look great, and I still wasn't sure if I could do it, but Todd saw me that way. He believed in me. He ran up next to me and continued to shout at me. I couldn't decide if that was encouraging or irritating. I didn't know whether to hug him or punch him. The way I was feeling it wouldn't take much to irritate me. However, I was SO glad to see Todd and then I saw his wife Ellen and then, finally Jennifer. They wanted to know where I'd been. Hmmm. Let's see. Shopping? Reading a good book? Lying by the pool? Not quite. I quickly tried to summarize the worst race day of my life in a few sentences. They had not been where I thought they would be because I had not been where I told them I would be, at the time I told them I'd be there. No matter, I had finally hooked up with folks who, through their love and encouragement, could help me finish.

They couldn't stay on the course with me for long, so after another minute or two, I was alone again…sort of. The marathon course passed through Kona and then out onto the same highway that we had biked on. All through Kona people lined the course watching and cheering. My stomach was finally starting to settle down a bit just as the sun was settling down on the horizon to my left. It was beautiful. What can compare with a Hawaiian sunset? Runners streamed past me having already run out to the turn-around point and now were coming into town to finish. Mile after mile crept by. No energy, but no muscle pulls or blisters either. All my time goals for this race had gone out the window many miles before. My finishing time wouldn't matter at all anymore. Finishing was all that counted. Finish. Just finish.

CHAPTER EIGHT

Never Race Alone

"Two are better than one…woe to him who is alone when he falls…" – Ecclesiastes 4:9-10

I have received the encouragement of people in many races, and it's always been a delight to do so. One summer I went up to southwestern Minnesota to compete in, what I believe must be the world's smallest triathlon. There were only nine competitors who showed up. This race was promoted in several national magazines, so I was astounded that only nine athletes were there. Gary and Jan, some friends of ours, went with Jennifer and me. At first I wasn't even thinking about how I would do, but soon after the swim started, I found myself in second place.

The first-place triathlete got out of the water ahead of me, but he had a very slow bike transition. Mine was quicker so I was out on the bike first. I was leading the race. This just does not happen. So there I was on my bike thinking, *This is a good feeling. This is great! I love this! I'm winning!*

Well, soon the man who had beaten me out of the water

came flying by me. He was a big man, with a very powerful lower body. I looked at his muscle rich legs when he went by and I just kind of shriveled on the spot.

Gary, Jan and Jen were watching and they were yelling for me. They drove around to different points on the course in the car, and every time I'd come by, they yell, "Keep going! C'mon! You can catch him! He's nothing! I was thinking, *Yeah, you get out here and try to catch him!*

I went by Gary once and he yelled, "Linc, he's not a runner." I thought, *How do you know that? You don't know this man at all.*

He seemed to hear my thoughts. He yelled. "He can't run! You'll catch him on the run!"

I thought, *Okay, if I can just keep him in sight, maybe I can catch him on the run.*

He was so far ahead that he was just a dot on the horizon. But Gary was right. He couldn't run worth a lick. I caught him on the run and I came away the winner of the race. It was very exciting, even if it was the world's smallest triathlon. The words of my three supporters gave me the encouragement I needed.

"Keep Going!!!"

I've received the encouragement of my faithful wife at many races and from good friends like Gary. Once we had the chance to have the roles reversed in a 50-mile run we did one beautiful fall in 1996. Gary threw up halfway through the race—which is not an encouraging thing to have happen–but we kept pressing on, and at 37.5 miles, his calves were cramping so badly that he really couldn't run anymore.

Now this was a 12 1/2-mile dirt trail in a canyon. It was an out-and-back course that we were to do twice, totaling 50 miles. We'd gone out, back and out, but still needed to go back—the last 12.5 miles. But since Gary couldn't run anymore, he told me, "All I can do is walk. Go on. You run ahead."

I said, "No way, Gary."

He said, "No, go on, I know you can still run."

I said, "No way. I'm with you." I wasn't going to leave him. And he said, "All I can do is walk."

I said, "Fine, then we'll walk. We've got about three and a half hours to make the deadline cut off, and I think we can walk it."

So I got about 10 feet ahead of him and said, "Now you stay right here and stay with me." And so we started walking. There were times when I would yell sort of negatively at him, "Come on, Gary. How bad do you want this? You've trained too hard to quit now. C'mon!"

And there were other times I would use more positive words, like, "Gary, come on man. Only four more miles. Come on! We're almost there. Keep coming. You can do it."

Gary later told me that without my encouragement, he probably wouldn't have made it. But with my encouragement, and lots of determination, he crossed the line and became an ultra marathoner.

Encouragement means so much, yet it is free. You can give someone encouragement, and it doesn't cost you anything; but it can mean the world to them. I've received encouragement and I've tried to give it. Both are a blessing.

Tom

I have a friend named Tom who had a very unusual thing happen to him when he was just 8 years old. He had a stroke. The medical people told Tom's parents that he would never be the same. He'd most likely not excel at school and would not be able to achieve anything in the physical/athletic arena. The stroke affected the right side of his body, limiting greatly the use of his right arm and, to a lesser degree, his right leg.

Today, Tom has a master's degree. He has done what many said he could never do. A few years ago, two of us went to Kansas City to be with Tom as he attempted the 26.2-mile Kansas City marathon. Due to the stroke and the affect it had on his leg, Tom has a great deal of problems with blisters. My friend and I were ready with several pairs of dry socks and lots of Vaseline. Every few miles Tom would sit down on the curb and we'd go to work on his feet, pulling off his shoes and socks, reapplying a fresh coat of lubricant, putting clean, dry socks on him and then his shoes. We looked like a mini Indy 500 pit crew.

Tom made it to the finish line in spite of a severe cramp hitting him at mile 23. Tom is a no-limits man. Maybe that's why I like being around him. He works as a school career counselor encouraging young people to discover their destinies. What a joy to encourage Tom that day all the way to the finish line.

A Father's Encouragement

Derek Redmond needed some encouragement in the 1992 Olympics. Running for Great Britain in a preliminary heat of the 400 meters, he felt a pop and a tug in his right hamstring muscle. He crumbled to the track in great pain, feeling like a dagger had been stuck into the back of his leg. In despair, he realized he was now out of the finals that would be held in 48 hours. His chances for a medal had vanished. His pain was greater than most would have felt because four years earlier in the Seoul Olympics he'd made it to the finals but had not been able to race due to an Achilles tendon injury. After four more years of hard training, here he was…lying on the track writhing in pain.

Though injured and out of the finals, he thought he'd at least try to finish. So, he picked himself up off the track and started to limp down the backstretch towards the final turn and the finish line. Derek saw a rotund man approaching him. The man grabbed the injured runner who began to cry in the man's arms. It was his father, Jim Redmond. His dad had been sitting among the upper rows of Olympic Stadium, and when he saw his son go down, he began making his way to the track. Guards tried to stop him.

"I wasn't going to be stopped," Jim Redmond said. Derek was shocked to see his dad on the track since he had no accreditation or passes to be there. As soon as Jim touched his son, Derek was disqualified. But no one seemed to care about the rules at that point. Derek's dad said, "I was thinking about getting him there (the finish line) so he could say he finished the semifinals." Derek stated, "I wasn't going to let any injury keep me from finishing the race. Whether people thought I was an idiot or whether people thought I was a hero, I was going to finish." And, with the encouragement and help of his father, he did.

Encourage Those Around You

Some people will not make it to the place God has for them without the encouragement from others. You don't know what the words you give somebody might mean to him or her. It might be the very difference in whether they get to the finish line or not.

Ecclesiastes 4:9-10 says, "Two are better than one, for if one falls, the other can lift up his friend, but woe to him who falls alone and has not someone to lift him up."

There are at least three groups of encouragers that need to be in your life. The first group is the "great cloud of witnesses." We read in Hebrews 11 about the heroes of faith, and we're encouraged. Though they're dead, their lives still speak powerfully to us. Others who have gone on to glory, such as grandparents, pastors and others who have influenced us, still encourage us by the trail of faithfulness they have left behind.

The second group could be called "encouragement friends." These are people who lift your spirit every time you're with them. There are people in my life who make me laugh every time I'm with them. There are others who speak destiny into my life. These are people who inspire me and "fill my tank" so to speak.

The third group is the most important and that is your accountability friends. These are the people who know the worst about you and still believe in you. They know your most private failures, private struggles and encourage you, pray for you and believe in you.

Some of you will not make it without accountability because the weaknesses that would keep you back are hidden. Until you are willing to put them out on the table with a trusted friend who you know loves you, you'll not make it. You have to be held accountable or it just won't happen. Fear and pride are often the two things that keep you from having an accountability friend. But you have to overcome fear and pride because you need accountability.

Don't run the race set before you alone. One of the cornerstones of success in this race is companionship–running together. What happens when a sheep wanders away from the Shepherd's eye and the company of the other sheep? He usually dies or is attacked by wolves. He needs the protection of others.

Review:

Principle # 1 – You Must Have a Plan
Principle # 2 – You Must Have a Sense of Pace
Principle # 3 – You Must Hydrate and Eat
Principle # 4 – You Must Protect Your Feet (Relationships)
Principle # 5 – Learn to Handle Pain, Setbacks and Failure
Principle # 6 – Develop a No-Limits Mentality
Principle # 7 – NEVER RACE ALONE

It was now completely dark as I jogged down the Queen K Highway. Every now and then I could see the bright NBC camera lights as they shot footage of those who pressed on through the night attempting to earn the prestigious "Iron-man" title. I could also see the lights at the aid stations along the route; but in between, I simply put one foot in front of the other and moved on through the darkness. I made the right-hand turn at mile 19 bringing me out of a place I mentioned earlier called the Natural Energy Lab. Interesting name for a place where hardly anyone has any energy left. With about seven miles left to go, I began to realize one reason the Lord had allowed me into this race.

I came upon a woman who was really struggling. She was walking, and as I came up to pass her, I asked her how she was doing. She said that she was not doing well at all. Her legs were cramping badly and she was losing it a little men-tally. She was trying to stay focused but was scrambling to hold it together. My heart went out to her. What a shame it would be for her to complete 2.4 miles of swimming, 112 miles of biking and 19 miles of the marathon only to be stopped just short of the finish line. As we talked I learned that her name was Marianne, that she was in her late 40s and that she was from Virginia. I told Marianne that I'd be glad for her and me to stay together, running when she felt up to it and walking when she needed to all the way to the finish if that would help. She agreed wholeheartedly. She then went on to tell me that she was recovering from cancer and her purpose for this race was to show that one could come all the way back from cancer and do an Ironman triathlon. Wow! What a lady! I told her she was amazing and I was honored to have met her.

She continued to labor on, questioning whether or not she could finish. I told her she was absolutely going to finish. We would finish together. I told her I was a pastor and asked if she'd like me to pray with her. She looked at me like I was the Apostle Paul and said, "Yes, please pray!" (Funny how open folks are to prayer at this point in an Ironman race.) As I began to pray, Marianne reached over and took my hand. Imagine this picture. Here I am walking down the Queen K Highway, in the dark, holding hands with a woman I had just met. As I prayed for her I was hoping that Jennifer and my friends wouldn't suddenly show up, or I'd have some explaining to do! The humor of the moment aside, I sensed the Lord's presence and a feeling of destiny in my meeting Marianne. We continued to press ahead, and I took every opportunity to encourage her, even praying a couple more times when she really needed it.

If you look up the Hawaiian Ironman 1998 final results, you'll see Marianne Raines listed as finishing in 1,249th place. That Christmas we sent her a Christmas card and she wrote a nice note back to us. She said her cancer had returned but that she was experiencing God's grace and had put her trust in Him. I discovered in late September of 2001 that Marianne had passed away just a week earlier on the 9th. She had put up a gallant four-year battle with a virulent form of breast cancer. I also learned she had been an elite athlete. She had represented the United States in '92, '93 and '95 at the International Amateur Triathlon Championships as well as competing in, and finishing, the Hawaiian Ironman in '94 and '96. Marianne was consistently ranked by "Triathlon Times" among the top five women Masters triathletes from 1991-1995. Amazingly, she had only begun taking up endurance sports in 1990.

After finishing the 1998 Ironman Triathlon, Marianne said, "I was not going to focus on what I couldn't do. I was going to focus on what I could do and work at that." Speaking of the cancer treatment she endured, she said, "I felt like an onion, and layer by layer by layer this disease was stripping away my dignity. I was slashed, scalped, burned and poisoned, but I swore I wouldn't let cancer touch my spirit, and running is what keeps me feeling in control."

She qualified for the Boston Marathon in 1998, just 10 days after a round of chemotherapy. Later, she completed the Boston run in three hours and 46 minutes, this time just three weeks after another round of chemotherapy. After the marathon she returned for radiation therapy.

She was as inspiring a person to be around as you can find. A friend of hers said, "I'm a crummy runner. But the only reason I run at all is because Marianne made me try. I used to see her at the pool, and she kept telling me I could do this. When I reluctantly started, she cheered my every step."

In speaking with a relative, he mentioned that Marianne had told him about our meeting in the '98 Ironman. She had told him that she didn't think she could have finished without me. You know, it truly is more blessed to give than to receive. God does work all things together for His good. The thigh pull and the winds had kept me from my time goals, causing me to be more than two hours behind schedule. But, they had allowed me to meet Marianne and see her to the finish line, which was much more meaningful than my own effort to get to the finish.

CHAPTER NINE
You Must Have Your Eyes Fixed on the Final Goal

"…run the race set before us, looking to Jesus…"
– Hebrews 12:1-2

Usually when I work out, I'm focusing on an upcoming race. Almost every time I swim, bike, run or lift weights, I'm thinking about that goal. That's one of the main reasons I exercise. That upcoming race is always on my mind.

Olympic athletes, who train the four years in between Olympics, think about the gold medal every day, every work-out. It's in their thoughts moment by moment.

For the mountain climber in training, the summit is the focus.

As Christians, we need to have the final goal fixed in our heart and in our eye. In Philippians 3:13-14, Paul said, "This one thing I do, forgetting what lies behind and straining toward what lies ahead, I press toward the goal for the prize of the upward call in Christ Jesus."

Later, and close to his death, Paul said, "I have finished the race. I have kept the faith." He said that because he had always kept in mind the goal of Christ. He saw Christ as his main goal, his finish line. He wanted to break the tape and finish strong.

John Stephen of Tanzania kept his focus on the final goal in the Mexico City Olympic marathon. Though he entered the stadium with a bloodied and bandaged right leg, finish he did…over an hour after the winner. When asked about his finish he said, "My country did not send me to Mexico City to start the race. They sent me here to finish the race."

Remember Those Before Us

"Since we are surrounded by so great a cloud of witnesses, let us run with endurance the race set before us, looking to Jesus, who for the joy set before Him…endured…" (Hebrews 12:1).

Maybe you're experiencing pain, setbacks or failure in your life. Maybe you've been tempted to quit trusting in God, but you feel the resolve in your heart to keep going through the pain and failure. You can be like the little boy in the poem who fell down three times but kept getting up. God is not fazed when you fall. He's still there, cheering you on and wanting to release in you the strength to continue and to finish.

Maybe you've limited yourself. You've limited what God can do in your life and you now want to throw off those limitations and let the great, unlimited Holy Spirit touch your heart afresh and anew and lead you into the amazing destiny that He has for you.

Maybe you realize that you need accountability in your life.

Perhaps you realize that you don't know God in a personal way, as your own loving Father. You need to decide today to start the race. Jesus can free you from the sin and chains that bind your heart.

Do you want to be a finisher in the race the Lord has placed before you? Do want to cross the finish line, whatever it takes?

Review:

Principle # 1 – You Must Have a Plan
Principle # 2 – You Must Have a Sense of Pace
Principle # 3 – You Must Hydrate and Eat
Principle # 4 – You Must Protect Your Feet (Relationships)
Principle # 5 – Learn to Handle Pain, Setbacks and Failure
Principle # 6 – Develop A No-Limits Mentality
Principle # 7 – Never Race Alone
Principle # 8 – HAVE YOUR EYES FIXED ON THE FINAL GOAL

The finish line. It's about the only thing that matters to the competitors in an Ironman race. When you're down to the last mile or two and you know you've made it, a little spring comes back into the step of even the weariest warrior. As I passed the marathon 25-mile marker and had 1.2 miles to go, a smile spread across my face. I made a right-hand turn, knowing I had but one more turn to make a block later, and I'd be able to see that which had been my focus for so many hours that day. I ran down the last small hill right next to Uncle Billy's Hotel where we had stayed, took that last right-hand turn and gazed down the last quarter mile of Hawaiian pavement to the finish. I had lived this scene many times before…but only in my mind and in my dreams.

I had watched ABC's first airing of the Hawaiian Ironman in 1982 when a completely exhausted Julie Moss had literally crawled the last few hundred yards to the finish line. Cruelly almost, the woman who had been in second place behind her had passed her just a few yards from the finish. I watched in amazement the incredible determination in Julie. Her legs were complete rubber. She tried to stand and walk, but her leg crumbled beneath her. All she could do was crawl, but the finish line called her name. She would not be denied. The Ironman credo is finish. Just finish. She crawled to it, touched it, and collapsed.

I tried to watch each year when the Hawaiian Ironman program was aired. I always thought I would love to give it a try, since I enjoyed running. There were, however, three major obstacles. First, there was the money. As a pastor, our needs were met, but we didn't have the financial resources to spend a week in Hawaii. Second, I really didn't think I could actually compete in a race of that magnitude. And, third, I had no way to get into the race. The vast majority of the 1,500 competitors gained entry into the Hawaiian race by being super fast in another qualifying race. I was not that fast. But, the Lord had provided another way into this incredible race that I know was divine. After I was accepted into the race, my grandmother paid my entry fee. Then Jen and I were able to use frequent-flier miles to fly there for almost nothing, and we were able to stay at an inexpensive but clean hotel. With these issues resolved, the only question left had been would I actually be able to finish? And here I was, looking at the final 400 yards that separated me from overcoming that third and final obstacle—completing the 140-mile course.

At this point, I saw the road was lined with thousands of people from many nations, all of them cheering wildly for each weary finisher. Then to my amazement they began to cheer for me! I saw the extremely bright NBC lights shining down on the final 200 yards that were covered with a long, green carpet. Waist-high barriers separated the spectators from the athletes and formed a gauntlet that led to a 20-foot high archway, which framed the finish line. I saw flags of many nations hanging from each side of the gauntlet, forming a canopy of beautiful colors. Music was playing and many were clapping and swaying to the beat as they celebrated. Each finisher, as they approached the carpet and ran the final 200 yards, heard their name called out over the huge sound system.

More than 1,300 names of finishers were called out that night before the midnight cutoff. Weary, battered, but joyful, each one had finished the course set before them. And now, they were receiving the respect and congratulations they had earned. I knew that I would never again have this experience, and so I slowed down and just took it all in. I heard my name called over the loud speakers, "Here comes Lincoln Murdoch from Omaha, Nebraska! Let's bring him in! Good job, Lincoln!" Seemingly, before I could blink, it was over. Ironman finisher.

A green lei of vines with maroon ribbons on it was placed around my neck. Jennifer was there to greet me and congratulate me with a hug and a kiss. My other friends waved and shouted congratulations from a distance. The one person used of the Lord to get me into the race was there as well. He congratulated me. I knew I hadn't qualified for this race. I shouldn't have been in it. I had done nothing to deserve it. It was through the kindness and love of another that I was able to run this race.

A beautiful Hawaiian Ironman finisher's medal was also put around my neck. I just stared at it. After 16 years of dreaming about competing in and finishing this race, it had happened. Because of God's grace and kindness, and through His strength, the dream was realized.

Conclusion

There is another, much more important race that every human being on the planet has been invited to participate in. God Himself has extended to each of us an opportunity to run this race. There is just one problem. None of us can qualify. Just as I wasn't good enough to qualify for the Hawaiian Ironman Triathlon and could only enter through the act of another person, in the same way, none of us are able to meet the qualifications for this race. I'm speaking of the race called The Christian Life. It's a race that brings forgiveness of sins and purpose and meaning in this life, with a guarantee of eternal life in heaven when we die. Most importantly though, this is not a race about us. It's about Him. It's about glorifying God by running this race for His honor and glory and running it through the power of His Spirit and not our own efforts.

The problem of getting into this race has nothing to do with not being able to swim, bike or run fast enough, nor does it have anything to do with not getting your name selected in the Ironman lottery. The problem is sin. Romans 3:23 says, "All have sinned and come short of the glory of God." How many sins does it take to fall short? James 2:10 tell us that if we break just one of God's commandments, just one time, we fail. And, the problem isn't that we don't get to go to Hawaii for a week. The problem is that we don't get to be in heaven, spending eternity with the Lord Jesus. Romans 6:23 says, "The wages or results of sin is death..." We just don't qualify.

How then do we get in to this most important race of all? God has made a way through His Son, Jesus, who took our place on the cross. We're the sinners, not Jesus. Yet, He took our place there to make a way for us to be cleansed of our sins (1 John 1:9) and become pure before God. This only happens when we are willing to admit that we are sinners in need of His forgiveness. Then we must repent, which is to make a spiritual U-turn, turning from running our own life and choosing to let Him run it. It's getting off the throne of our life and letting Him take His rightful place there as Lord and Savior.

There is one problem many people have and that is they're not willing to surrender their will. They might *believe* that all of the above is true, but until they are willing to vacate the driver's seat of their life and get into the backseat, nothing changes. If you're on a sinking ship, you might believe all the right things about the lifeboat; but until you actually get into it, you'll not be saved. Some people will miss heaven by 12 inches, which is the distance from our head to our heart.

Someday, those who have waved the white flag of their life and surrendered to the Lordship of Jesus will make that last turn on the course of this life. They'll look at the great finish line that leads to heaven. There'll be countless others there who have finished before them. That group will be from every nation on the Earth, just like the flags in Hawaii. There won't be any need for NBC lights because the book of Revelation tells us that the glory of God is heaven's light and it's lamp is the Lamb, Jesus. Hebrews 12 tells of the great group of others who witness our race. I can imagine them cheering each and every one in as they run that final, glorious gauntlet and hear their name called out. Names from Russia, Bolivia, Malaysia, Siberia, Turkmenistan, Chile, Vietnam, Finland, China, Italy, the United States, and every other nation. When the believers cross the finish line, they'll see Jesus, and with gratitude too deep to express, they'll give their finisher medal to Him because He is the One who deserves it and the only One worthy of it.

If you've made this decision, then you know and have the assurance that this is true and applies to you. If you haven't made this decision, which is the most important decision you'll ever consider making, then please look at the last section of this book to see just where you are and what is next for you.

Whatever you do, don't quit. If you know Jesus in a real and personal way, then keep running, looking to Jesus, the Author and Finisher of your faith. Run to the very end and say with the Apostle Paul, "I have finished the race. I have kept the faith." If you don't know Him this way, then keep searching because you are promised in His Word that those who search for Him will find Him. I pray the principles in this book will help you along your way. Let's make a deal. If you get to heaven's finish line before I do, when you hear my name called out will you come and cheer me in? If I recognize your name, I promise I'll do the same for you. See you at the finish!

Step Up to Life

**Life on Earth is like a game . . . it has a start and a finish.
Find where you are in the "game of life"!**

Step 1:
Unconcerned

**We all start here. You may know a lot about Jesus
or very little. You may even respect Him.
The real point is, you don't really care about
a personal relationship with Him.**

Step 2:
Concerned

**You're sensing emptiness, dissatisfaction or even fear.
You know there's more to life than what you're
experiencing. What is life all about? Why am I here?
What you need are spiritual answers.**

Step 3:
Convicted

**You are uncomfortable because your lifestyle is
causing guilt or emptiness. Selfish "please me" choices
are sinful and break not only God's Ten Commandments,
but eventually yourself. God's passing grade on goodness
is keeping the Ten Commandments perfectly in thought,
word and deed. You have failed and you're bothered.**

Step 4:
Repentant

You agree you have lived a life based on your choices with Christ left out. You now turn from your way to His way, from your management to His. Jesus said "unless you repent you will all perish." Luke 13::3

Step 5:
Committed to the Lord Jesus Christ

You give Jesus Christ your life and the right to run it. He gives you His life and meaning for living. You receive Jesus Christ and take His death as payment for you sins. God receives you as His own child and puts His Son's life within you (Galatians 4:4-6). He also forgives you and prepares a place for you in heaven. "Believe in the Lord Jesus Christ and you shall be saved." Acts 16:31

S E E   Y O U   A T   T H E
Finish!

Where are you?

- ☐ I am uncommitted
- ☐ I am thinking about making a commitment
- ☐ I am committing myself now to Jesus Christ
  and will seek to obey Him daily.

For Additional Resources:
www.crosstrainingpublishing.com